Wild Weather

By Sean McCollum
Illustrated by Jesse Graber

Library For All Ltd.

Library For All is an Australian not for profit organisation with a mission to make knowledge accessible to all via an innovative digital library solution. Visit us at libraryforall.org

Wild Weather

This edition published 2022

Published by Library For All Ltd
Email: info@libraryforall.org
URL: libraryforall.org

Library For All gratefully acknowledges the contributions of all who made previous editions of this book possible.

This is an adaption of an original work developed by the USAID and licensed under the Creative Commons Attribution 3.0 IGO License. Views and opinions expressed in the adaption are the sole responsible for the author or authors of the adaption and are not endorsed by USAID.

FROM THE AMERICAN PEOPLE

Original illustrations by Jesse Graber

Wild Weather
McCollum, Sean
ISBN: 978-1-922835-34-5
SKU02727

Wild
Weather

Look outside. Is the sun shining? Is the wind blowing? Is rain falling from the clouds? There are many kinds of weather.

The weather is always changing. It might be hot or cool. It might be wet or dry. Sometimes weather gets wild. Different places in the world have different kinds of wild weather.

Rain Storms

In Liberia, rain storms are a kind of wild weather. Dark clouds gather. Lightning flashes in the sky. Thunder booms. The rain falls very hard. Strong winds make the trees dance. Everything gets wet.

Dust Storms

Some parts of Africa are very dry. Dry dirt turns into dust. Wind lifts the dust into the sky. People cover their faces. This wild weather is called a dust storm.

Cyclones

Some big storms start over the ocean. Their clouds turn in big circles. They are called cyclones. Some people call them hurricanes. Their winds are very, very strong. They bring lots of rain. People stay dry inside until this wild weather stops.

Tornadoes

In some parts of the world, big rain storms can cause tornadoes. Tornadoes are clouds that spin very fast. They are powerful and can knock down houses. People hide until this wild weather passes.

Snow Storms

Some places can be very cold. Rain turns into white snow. Cold winds blow the snow around. It gets deeper and deeper. People put on coats to stay warm. They wear boots, too. They might throw snowballs in this wild weather.

Weather Science

Scientists study the weather. They check the temperature with a thermometer. They measure how much rain falls. Then they let us know what the weather will be today. They might tell us what the weather will be tomorrow. These reports help us know what to wear to school. They might tell us to bring a jacket or an umbrella in case of rain.

Climate

Scientists look for weather patterns that show the weather from year to year. These patterns are called climate. What is the climate like in Liberia? It is often hot. The rainy season usually starts in May and ends in October.

Today, scientists say the climate is changing. Our world is getting warmer. They also think our wild weather is getting wilder.

You can use these questions to talk about this book with your family, friends and teachers.

What did you learn from this book?

Describe this book in one word. Funny? Scary? Colourful? Interesting?

How did this book make you feel when you finished reading it?

What was your favourite part of this book?

About the contributors

Library For All works with authors and illustrators from around the world to develop diverse, relevant, high quality stories for young readers. Visit libraryforall.org for the latest news on writers' workshop events, submission guidelines and other creative opportunities.

Did you enjoy this book?

We have hundreds more expertly curated original stories to choose from.

We work in partnership with authors, educators, cultural advisors, governments and NGOs to bring the joy of reading to children everywhere.

Did you know?

We create global impact in these fields by embracing the United Nations Sustainable Development Goals.

libraryforall.org

www.ingramcontent.com/pod-product-compliance
Lightning Source LLC
Chambersburg PA
CBHW040321050426
42452CB00018B/2951